# NO

## M O R E

# STRESS

# NO
MORE
STRESS

Design and creation: GRAPH'M

ISBN: 2-7528-0090-8
Publisher code: T00090

Copyright registration: September 2004
Printed in Singapore by Tien Wah Press

www.fitwaypublishing.com
Fitway Publishing
12, avenue d'Italie – 75627 Paris cedex 13

# NO
## MORE
# STRESS

delphine barbier sainte marie
illustrations alain bouldouyre

# Contents

# INTRODUCTION

## NO MORE STRESS

Can't get up in the morning? Feel like killing everyone as soon as you get behind the wheel of your car? Do you have frustrating sexual problems that make you feel even more dissatisfied and make you act like a bear with a sore head all day? And – tick the right box – do you take refuge in a frenzy of cigarettes, chocolate bars, cups of strong coffee? Do you feel permanently under attack as if the whole world is gunning for you – from your car breaking down to the miserable weather (It's raining again … just not fair, right?)

You are one of the 28 per cent of professionals in Europe who complain of feeling stressed at work*. This means 44 million people whose unhappiness at work makes them feel out of sorts. In Canada, the figure is around double that amount. On top of ever more demanding workloads and increasing uncertainty over job security, we have to deal with a declining quality of life – pollution, traffic jams, relationship anxiety, resource cuts, personal dissatisfaction and feelings of inadequacy. Stress can invade every area of your life.

> **STRESS: A FACTOR TO BE TAKEN INTO ACCOUNT …**
> People under stress are:
> – **Three times more likely to suffer from stress-related illnesses.**
> – **Twice as likely to resign from their jobs.**
> – **Twice as likely to suffer from professional 'burnout'.**
> – **Twice as likely to regularly work overtime.**
> (North Western National Life Company, 1992)

# NO
## MORE
## STRESS

Now stop! Don't wait until you have an ulcer, a bad back, sleeping difficulties or depression; let's tackle it now, and the first thing to do is to take a deep breath.

Take one minute: that's the amount of time you need to relax. Do you have three minutes? Even better. Can you free up an hour? Three times better.

This little guide wants to be your friend. Do you want to know how you can cheer yourself up and revitalise your body at the same – all in one minute? How you can release stress-related knots in a week? How you can avoid being driven to distraction by your monthly schedule? How you can understand how your body works in order to manage levels of stress in the long term? This book is your friend. There are no complicated theories: just simple, easy activities, tricks and tips from people just like you; and advice from experts to help you tackle stress effectively.

> **... WHICH HAS A SOCIAL COST:**
> **UK: 3 bn £**
> **USA: 21 bn US$**
> **In general: between 2 and 4 % of GDP.**
> *(ILO 2000)*

*According to a survey carried out in the year 2000 by the European agency for health and safety at work.

# What is stress exactly?

Before we start, you should know that stress is a perfectly normal bodily reaction. Psychologist Hans Selye, who introduced the term to medicine, describes it as 'the body's nonspecific response to a demand placed on it'.

In simpler language, this means that the body has a way of responding to any situation that is unknown, surprising, unforeseen or even dangerous. This 'alarm system' is an instinctive response that helps us to perform well in a difficult situation and react appropriately to a dangerous one.

The body's response also varies, depending on whether the stress is short-lived or ongoing.

In case of a short-lived stress:

**1st phase of alert:** the hypothalamus activates the nervous system and the adrenal glands secrete the hormone adrenaline.

**2nd phase:** immediate action which involves two possible responses – fight or flight.

*In the EU, more than half of lost working days are the result of stress.*

During this time, the body shows symptoms of the stress: palpitations, sweating, stomach pains, muscular spasms, cold hands and feet. This is because the body is focusing on getting oxygen to the brain and the muscles.

In case of an ongoing stress:

1st **phase:** the hypothalamus activates both the blood system and the adrenal glands which release cortisol.

2nd **phase:** gradual action. The aim is to stimulate the production of glucose to give the body energy to fight, and to boost the immune system to protect against infections and reduce pain and fever.

However, certain levels of stress can be unhealthy. This 'bad' stress appears 'when there is an imbalance between the perception that a person has of the demands of his environment and his perception of his ability to deal with them.' ** So there you are. Unhealthy levels of stress will affect your physical health and may lead to panic attacks, anxiety, weakened immune system, the onset of diabetes, high blood pressure or even to depression or a heart attack.

**According to the European agency for health and safety at work.

# Recognising the symptoms

*More than a third of the working population regularly receive confusing or contradictory instructions (35%).*

✓ A negative view of yourself and of others – you are dissatisfied and you feel like a victim; you may feel guilty, let-down, bitter, misunderstood, neglected or rejected. Your behaviour is self-absorbed, and can even be aggressive and violent.

✓ Inability to cope at work – increasing job insecurity and fear of redundancy are high stress factors. You may feel that you are being left behind, or that you are swamped by unrealistic deadliness. You may feel you are not grasping anything any more and that you have difficulties expressing your opinion. You may find it difficult to take criticism or have a problem saying 'no'. Middle managers are often most affected because they have pressure from senior managers above them and also from the teams working under them. However, stress can affect any employee subjected to current

management methods that empha-sise individual performance and the importance of meeting targets.

✓ Finally, stress levels may start to cause physical ailments (for example, stomach pains, backache or insom-nia) and a visit to your doctor is the only possible solution. Your doctor will be able to identify whether it is a short-lived episode or a more seri-ous chronic condition.

**One worker in three complains of stress from contact with the general public (30%).**

*More than one worker in two has his working pattern imposed on him in order to satisfy a request immediately (54%).*

**NO** MORE STRESS

# Work-related stress

### 10 pieces of advice to avoid 'burnout'

1- Build time into your schedule for unforeseen events.
2- Don't try to do several tasks at the same time.
3- Avoid taking on other colleagues' problems.
4- Don't be scared of saying 'no'.
5- Put off responding to e-mails and phone calls in order to give yourself time to think.
6- Delegate some of your duties so you can focus on important tasks.
7- Acknowledge that time lost explaining a task will be won back later.
8- Make short- and medium-term goals to motivate yourself.
9- Plan times and places to interact with other employees.
10- Regularly re-assess your position and objectives with your boss.

*(Source: Gereso, an HR company)*

*More than one worker in two works in a highly pressurised job (52%).*

*Nearly one quarter of workers have unrealistic deadlines (23%).*

## Learn to recognise your false friends, the 'pollutants'.

The mobile phone has changed your life, e-mail has changed the way you work: well, yes, but is it for the better? Our culture of immediacy; the 'straightaway', 'now', 'get this done yesterday' culture is a powerful stress factor. Is it a good idea to work with your telephone receiver wedged under your chin, as you write an e-mail and signal to someone else who can't wait for you to finish your phone conversation? You will work more efficiently if you protect your time and space – plan your priorities (open the post after your first task), decide what is important and urgent (prepare for the meeting before doing the memo for George) and arrange a meeting for later with the person you are speaking to. Very often, this will mean that things don't develop into problems in the first place.

## My tip for managing my time

*Hervé, 38, Senior Civil Servant.*

'The hardest thing is establishing a balance between the quality of work I have to produce and the time it takes me to do it. You have to accept that you cannot be everywhere all the time. And you always need to move on to the next task. Who cares if you are made to look ridiculous in a meeting? You'll be better in another one. I always check with my colleagues how urgent the files they send me are. Two thirds of 'urgent' files aren't urgent at all. As for orders from my boss, I make sure I distinguish what is urgent and what is important. I must admit that I do like to play games with stress (I work out catastrophic scenarios), then it's me who is in charge of the process.'

13

# Test: What stress

*This test will help you work out how this book can be of use to you.*

### 1- IT IS MONDAY MORNING. HOW ARE YOU FEELING AS YOU START YOUR WORKING DAY?

**a)** You spent the weekend mulling over the problems that you have to tackle and you charge at them with your head down.

**b)** You say a brief hello to your colleagues and discuss your priorities with your assistant.

**c)** You start by drinking a cup of coffee at the machine to help clear your head and discuss the weekend with your work mates.

### 2- AN EMERGENCY MEETING IS CALLED AND YOU HAVE TO BE THERE. HOW DO YOU FEEL?

**a)** More lost time! You are raging internally, and you spend the meeting with your head in your files and one eye on the clock.

**b)** This is going to mean more overtime and you arrive at the meeting glowering at everyone, making it clear that you don't want to be there.

**c)** You delegate the task you are working on and head for the meeting, having decided not to spend any more than an hour there, even if it means leaving while it's still going on.

# ype are you?

**3-** **O**N **F**RIDAY AT MIDDAY, A RANDOM CLIENT WANTS TO CHANGE AN ENTIRE FILE WHICH HAS TO GO TONIGHT. **H**OW DO YOU REACT?

**a)** You go red in the face and shout down the phone that he has had all month to check your proposals, and you slam down the phone on the incompetent idiot.

**b)** You try to reason with him in vain, and attempt to propose a compromise. Your week-end is ruined and the only thing you can do is hope for a miracle.

**c)** Given what's at stake, you tell him that you will have to refer the matter to your superior, who is the only one that can decide what action to take. You leave for your weekend on time.

**4-** **Y**OUR BOSS HAS OFFERED YOU A PROMOTION, WHICH MEANS A SIGNIFICANT INCREASE IN YOUR WORKLOAD, AND PROMISES TO FIND YOU AN ASSISTANT SOON. **H**OW DO YOU FEEL?

**a)** You are sick at the very thought of what your days are going to be like in the future but you do not want to disappoint your boss, who is finally giving you the recognition you deserve.

**b)** You chase up the arrival of the assistant, weigh up your new responsibilities and ask to be relieved of certain tasks to compensate.

**c)** You tell your boss that this isn't going to work: it's the equivalent of two jobs and will require an extraordinary team, an increased budget and a much more substantial salary.

**5- It's up to you to implement the company's new strategy: you have to reduce the amount spent on wages and increase productivity.**

  **a)** You storm into your superior's office: 'Who are you kidding? How am I supposed to do this, then – work miracles?'

  **b)** You start to break out in a cold sweat and your heartbeat increases, faced with this 'mission impossible'. But you can't just break down. Who could you possibly talk to?

  **c)** You force yourself to think it through carefully. You send a memo to your superiors, explaining why the strategy is unrealistic, making it clear that you can't be responsible in the event of failure.

**6- How do you feel about the weekend?**

  **a)** Phew! It's a chance to sleep and eat – and I don't want to see anyone.

  **b)** Hmmm, it'll be nice as long as the children let us sleep.

  **c)** Yee ha! I can't wait for Saturday night.

**7- At home, it's time to put the kids to bed. You try once, twice, three times, but they just don't seem to speak the same language. How do you react?**

  **a)** You start sobbing like a baby.

  **b)** Oh, forget it! You slam the bedroom door behind you. It's not your job to look after her children.

  **c)** You suggest a race – the first one into bed with teeth brushed, and face and hands washed, gets a story.

**8-** WHEN YOU GET HOME IN THE EVENING, ALL
YOU WANT TO DO IS:
   **a)** Switch off completely in front of the TV.
   **b)** Talk to your partner about your worries.
   **c)** Relax and unwind. Talking about work is not
   allowed at home.

**9-** YOU FEEL THAT YOUR WIFE WANTS TO TALK.
HOW DO YOU RESPOND?
   **a)** You turn the volume up on the TV.
   **b)** You decide to take the rubbish out.
   **c)** You only half listen to what she is saying.

**10-** IN BED, YOUR GIRLFRIEND IS GETTING
TOUCHY-FEELY. HOW DO YOU FEEL?
   **a)** You're always scared of this moment. Last
   time, it was a complete disaster. What's more,
   you really don't feel like it.
   **b)** You yawn and offer her a classic 'cold shoulder'.
   **c)** Sex is just what you need, your adrenaline
   is pumping.

# Count up your answers.

### IF THE MAJORITY OF YOUR ANSWERS WERE a)
#### THIS BOOK IS MADE FOR YOU.

You are on the edge of a nervous breakdown. You get murderous tendencies as soon as you get behind the wheel of your car and you can smoke a packet of cigarettes without even realising. In the morning, you can't work out why: 1) you find it so difficult to get up even though you have two alarm clocks, 2) coffee no longer has any effect, 3) everyone keeps hiding your stuff. It is at times like these that you are asked to do unbelievably inconvenient things like posting a letter, taking the little one to school or writing a cheque for the taxman. 'Do you realise how much I have on?' you scream at your partner. Why has she got it in for you? And the day hasn't even started. Stop! At this rate, you won't be able to cope with your job or with family life. You are literally 'dis-connecting' – you have lost all sense of perspective, you are losing a grip on your job, and even those who love you find you impossible to live with. You are self-destructing.

### IF THE MAJORITY OF YOUR ANSWERS WERE b)
#### THIS BOOK IS ALSO MADE FOR YOU.

Your stress type sticks his head in the sand. You would rather run away than face problems. You let yourself get drowned by your problems and by the contradictory orders of your superiors. Any responsibilities are burdens, and any goals are impossible. You know very well that you are heading straight for the wall, or, in any case, that's what you think. You can't sleep and you take no pleasure in anything. You have heartburn, cold sweats as soon as arrive at work, and your heart pounds when your boss says he wants to see you. When Sunday night comes, you feel ill at the thought of what awaits you the next day, but you can't talk about it. No one can help you, not even yourself. You are at a dead-end and you feel as if you are trapped in a room with the roof slowly lowering to crush you. Rather than ask for help, you are paralysed by panic. The crash is coming soon. And what's more, you are waiting for it to happen as if it is going to be a relief.

## IF THE MAJORITY OF YOUR ANSWERS WERE c)
### YOU WERE MADE FOR THIS BOOK.

You are stressed and you know you are. You try to deal with situations to the best of your ability even if that requires an immense effort. You have realised that the only way of pulling through is to talk and to break the wall of silence. You are determined to swim, not sink, and you are going to say when enough really is enough. Not bad. But sometimes, while you are hoping for that good stress to spur you on, you slip into panic. You are tired of battling in a storm, your hand clinging to the helm of the boat, with big waves splashing in your face. If only you could find a calm refuge. Help is at hand – it only takes a few simple steps.

**NO**
M O R E

# Your body is a

*And before you throw
yourself into a big
fitness campaign that
you will give up
after a few weeks,
you must … stop.
Your body has
some secrets to
share with you.*

20

# temple, you know

You're not the only person who has failed to understand that the body and soul need to be taken as a whole. If you pay for an hour's massage, thinking that it will be a good opportunity to decide on the best way of asking your boss for a pay rise, forget it. That is pointless, a waste of time and money.

Are you already scoffing and telling yourself that you don't have time for this sort of silliness? If so, you're wrong. Managing stress can only begin if you are aware that you are simply human and that like all human beings, you have limits that you shouldn't stretch unless you want to risk an American-style 'burnout' or *karoshi,* as they say in Japan. So, this book offers tried and tested techniques from experts, and hints and tips from people who have been subjected to great stress. There are exercises, postures and stretches that you can practise, and all you need is the motivation to try them out. You will find that the physical benefits are immediate, but don't expect a permanent quick-fix. You must practise regularly. At this early stage, we are just aiming for awareness, and that's just the beginning.

# Have you got a minute?

Our bodies have a range of natural, instinctive actions that are very effective anti-depressants – one hundred per cent biological, built-in and with no nasty side effects. Here are the techniques, 'tried and tested' by our experts:

## I
## Laughing

In your car, in the shower, while you're watching TV, at the dinner table, in public or in private. In short, get your zygomatics going. You will feel better: it's a fact. According to Bernard Raquin, a leading light in the world of 'laughter therapy', 'forced laughter can be a mental and physical cleansing process because it has the same effect as spontaneous laughter.' Physically, the diaphragm starts moving, which in turn stimulates the circulation and improves the supply of oxygen to the brain. Yes, but how exactly do you do it? 'You need to breathe in and out, in short breaths, and build up the rhythm. This provides the body with more oxygen. Then comes the panting, which resembles the muffled cry of the marmoset. Then there is nothing left to do but to let out the 'ha ha', which will enable you to open your mouth and get your stomach muscles working.'

***The benefits:*** *relaxes the body and the soul,*

*and puts you in a good mood. This should be done ten times a day.*

# 2
## Singing

This has the same effect on the body as laughing. Basically, this is one of the few times that you really open your mouth wide. The diaphragm lifts and expands and deep respiration (breathing) begins, which improves the body's oxygen supply. Singing badly works just as well!

***The benefits:*** *improved respiration that increases the oxygen supply to the brain.*

# 3
## Yawning

Contrary to what you may have been told when you were little, it's good to yawn. It's a sign that you are releasing tension; it says, 'I feel good', 'I am relaxing'.

***The benefits:*** *it's a super-quick relaxation technique if you are careful to stretch properly, like a cat, and to hold the posture for a few seconds. If you focus on your breathing, you will feel relaxed and calm.*

# 4
## Shouting or screaming

We advise you to do this at home with all the doors shut, or in your car on the motorway. Whether it is primal or not, the scream is a psychological cleanser of the nervous system and acts as an effective safety valve.

***The benefits:*** *it's a release!*

# 5
## Listening to music

All the experts will tell you that listening to Mozart is a stimulant, while techno music, which subjects the body to rapid vibrations, is a depressant.

*The benefits: hospitals have been using music therapy for 20 years to treat anxiety, insomnia and even depression. Music helps the patient to reconnect with the world and to relax.*

# 6
## Walking on a reflexology mat

These mats are made of plastic and are covered with rounded points. They are available from pharmacies. You can use it to massage your feet while you are brushing your teeth or shaving.

*The benefits: this stimulates the reflex points and maintains the digestive system.*

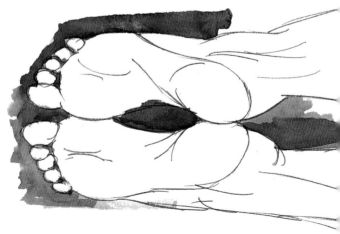

## 7
## Stretching your toes

This is a reflexology movement. Take hold of each toe in turn pulling and stretching it gently in a clockwise direction.

**The benefits**: *this technique relaxes the head. In this ancient Chinese therapy, the 7,200 nerve endings of the feet represent different areas of the body.*

## 8
## Kneading the solar plexus

Push in a clockwise direction in the middle of the arch of the foot. It is very important that you do this on both sides.

**The benefits**: *frees up the digestive system (intestines, colon).*

1
min

NO
M O R E
STRESS

# 9
# Finding your stress ball

Found between the big toes and the second toes, this 'stress ball' should be massaged to release tension.

***The benefits:*** *this point can be very sensitive and, once massaged, will relax the neck.*

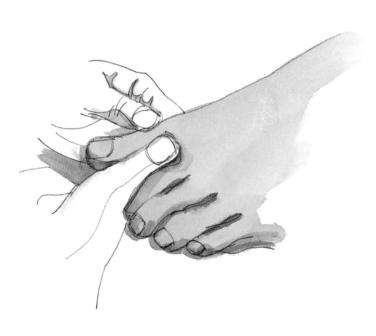

# 10
## Stretching the ear

Pinch and pull gently along your ear lobe, holding it between your thumb and forefinger. In reflexology, this is called 'working on the door of the ear'. Next massage the inner corner of the ear, and then press again on the 'door' itself with small movements.

*Massaging the inner ear relates to the spinal column.*

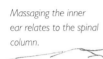

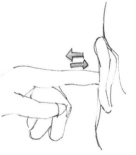

*The vibrations go straight to the brain. Massaging this reflex area, which is linked to the brain, allows you to revitalise your cerebral functions.*

*Pinch the ears with a circular motion until you get to the bottom.*

# NO
### MORE
## STRESS

## 'I condition myself mentally.'
*Hervé, 38, Senior Civil Servant.*

**I build walls:** 'I make a clear separation between my work and my home. As I cross the doorstep of my house, I condition myself to close my mind to any thoughts about work.'

**I protect my sleep:** 'I have a method of getting to sleep by surrounding myself with positive thoughts. I even forbid my wife to talk about things that are worrying her in bed'.

**I infuse:** 'I treat my heartburn with an infusion of star anise, fennel, green aniseed and papaya that I buy in health food shops.'

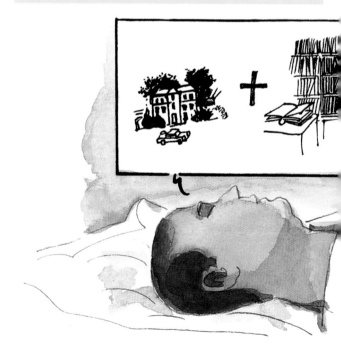

# NO
M O R E
## STRESS

1
min

## My tip for getting to sleep

*Hervé, 38, Senior Civil Servant.*

'I think back to my childhood, when I was happy, and imagine myself revisiting the house in the most minute detail. I rummage around in the library, I look behind the curtains, I open drawers … this works immediately. You can also apply this to parts of the body. You start at the feet and, inch by inch, you move up to the roots of your hair. Usually, you don't have time to get to the head.'

# Breathing

Relaxation is based on breathing, concentration and an awareness of each part of the body and its different functions. Learn to breathe deeply in order to cleanse your body, to protect yourself, to put things in perspective, and to distance yourself from whatever is annoying you.

## Yoga

Yoga, which is the basis for all relaxation techniques, helps you to behave and move in a completely different way: 'slowly, calmly and with awareness', as Jean-François de Righetti, a relaxologist and yoga professor puts it. 'All violent sports have the opposite effect of what is needed and provoke tensions. Be aware that the body cleanses and detoxifies itself 70 per cent by breathing, 28 per cent by filtration organs such as the liver and the kidney and 2 per cent by sweating … and breathing acts like a therapeutic massage for the heart, chest and stomach, which are very sensitive to stress.'

### The principle:

Hatha Yoga signifies the union (yoga) of the sun (ha) and the moon (tha). Yoga is a slow, gentle therapy that can lead to meditation and relaxation. It is based on the principle of

30

balancing the body's energy. The aim is to learn to breathe properly, to focus your energy and to rebalance it. Yoga originated in India and is based on the principles of energy flow found in traditional Chinese medicine. A man in good health is a man whose energy is flowing around his body without blockages or imbalances, and this brings together yin (the feminine element, the moon) and yang (the masculine element, the sun). Yoga helps you to manage stress by using breathing techniques.

A complete breath can be broken down into three levels: abdominal, thoracic and subclavian. Once you have got the knack, the aim is to link these three levels of breathing in a wave motion that rises and falls.

How do you breathe in yoga? Well, not like you and me!

## 'Let go'

*Jean-François de Righetti, relaxologist.*

'Before you even begin your breathing exercises, the first thing to do is to focus on which parts of your body are tense. Your mind speaks gruffly while your body has a tiny voice, and you need to listen carefully. How? By focusing on your thoughts. Like clouds that you watch in the sky but can't hold on to. Close your eyes to create a void like a blank cinema screen.'

**The benefits:** *this exercise will help to calm your mind by discovering your body.*

## Exercise 1
## Shavasana, the corpse pose

Lie on your back so that you are aware of your body and can identify areas of tension. The rib cage must be open, so your arms should be stretched out with your palms towards the ceiling, your legs relaxed and slightly apart. The chin should be slightly forward to stretch the neck vertebrae. You are ready to begin exercise 2.

*You are in an infinite desert, with the Pyramids in front of you.*
### DO NOT GO TO SLEEP!

*Palms towards the ceiling.*

**5 mins**

## Exercise 2
## Puff out your chest

This breathing technique, which comes naturally to babies (instinctive yoga masters), involves breathing through your nose. It allows the rib cage to lift, which in turn causes the lungs to expand. When you breathe in, your diaphragm moves down; when you breathe out, the diaphragm pushes up towards the lungs and the chest deflates.

***The benefits****: for combatting stress, abdominal breathing is very important. The first signs of stress – spasms in the diaphragm – can be felt in the stomach.*

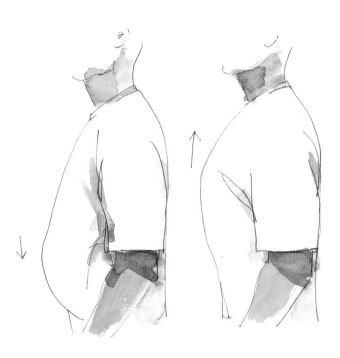

## Exercise 3
# Nadichodan

Focus on breathing through your nostrils one at a time. Breathe in with the right nostril (for invigorating yang) and breathe out with the left nostril (for calming yin). Then swap the order of breathing: breathe in with the left nostril and out with the right.

**The benefits:** *calms and rebalances … but only if you slow your breathing down as much as possible.*

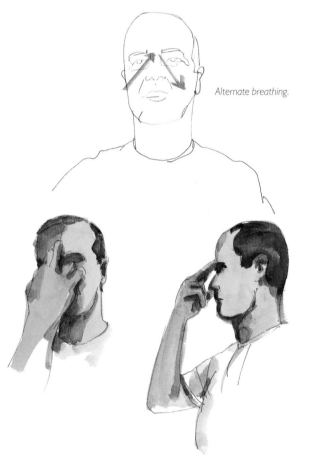

*Alternate breathing.*

## Exercise 4
## 'The boat'

In the corpse pose, tense your whole body as you breathe in. Then release, relaxing as you breathe out. Repeat three or four times.

**The benefits:** *for real nervous wrecks, a super-quick way to relax.*

↙ *Fists tightly clenched.*

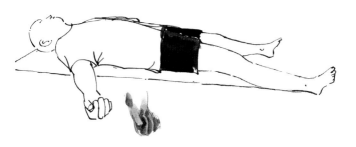

*The boat.*

## My tip for preparing for an important meeting
**(a quick-fix way to relax)**

*Hervé, 38, Senior Civil Servant.*

'You need to empty your mind of any thoughts. This is an exercise I do on the bus with beads but anything that has ten notches will do the trick. With my eyes closed, I recite a poem by heart ten times while breathing in through the nose and breathing out through the mouth. You need to focus on the meaning of each phrase, so the poem should only have about a dozen verses, not too long. This meditation exercise should last about 5 minutes.'

## My tip for relaxing after a stressful day

*Patrick, 41, is a soldier, formerly responsible within special forces.*

'Before we went into action, I used to get an adrenaline high followed by a low, which meant I found it difficult to manage the days following our operations. I used to have problems sleeping and wasn't hungry. My experience of martial arts taught me to harness and recharge my body energy levels by modifying my breathing. Sitting down or standing in a corner, I close my eyes and focus on my abdominal breathing: I breathe in deeply and I breathe out, visualising all my negative thoughts flying away. You should do this for 10 minutes during the day and then once for 15 minutes before you go to bed.'

# Relaxation

## Schültz's training

Doctor Schültz, who was a pupil of Freud, developed a range of relaxation exercises. You can do this ore wherever and whenever you want, visualising each part of your body as it is mentioned:

I am sitting comfortably behind my desk. My eyes are closed, I am completely calm.

1- My arms are heavy.
2- My hands are warm.
3- My heart is beating calmly and regularly.
4- I am relaxing to the rhythm of my breathing.
5- My solar plexus is warm.
6- I am imagining a breath of cool air on my forehead.

To finish the session: I breathe three times with my arms folded.

# Do-In: do-it-yourself shiatsu

This is a form of shiatsu, a technique that was conceived in Japan and has its roots in Chinese medicine. Based on the principle that the body is criss-crossed by 12 meridians (energy channels), shiatsu uses the same points worked on in acupuncture but uses finger pressure, not needles. Do-in, as its name (in Japanese) suggests, is a self-massage. You do not need to be a great shiatsuchi to treat yourself to a moment of relaxation.

Here are four simple movements, that you can do at work without people around you wondering if you have lost your marbles.

## 1- Stretch

Sitting up straight in a chair, grab the back of your neck with your hand. Press, stretch and gently manipulate the neck muscles. Repeat this movement at the top, the middle and the base of your neck.

NO MORE STRESS

**5 mins**

# 2- Relax

Still sitting in a chair, grab your right shoulder muscle and stretch and press it firmly towards the front of your shoulder. Release and repeat three times before doing the same thing with the left shoulder.

*Do-In: self-massage that can be done everywhere, as often as you like.*

## 3- Release

Stand up, with your legs slightly apart (you might need to make sure that no one is going to come into your office!). Apply gentle pressure to your waist around your hip bones. Move across to the middle of your back and apply pressure on both sides of the spinal column.

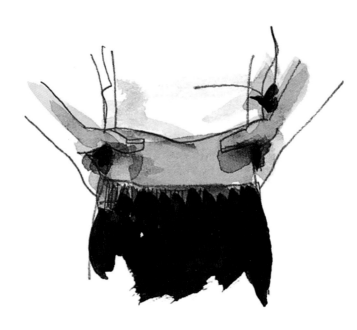

## 4- Revitalise

Tap lightly with your hand on the top of your head. Grab handfuls of hair and pull gently all over your head, or tap gently with your fist. Vary the intensity and the frequency of these actions.

*Raindrops.*

## Have you got 30 minutes?

# Yoga Nidra
## 30 minutes of sleep that will feel like an hour and a half

According to Jean-François de Righetti, this yoga technique, which means 'psychic sleep', is equivalent to a deep sleep of an hour and a half.

'It's about detaching your mind. The aim is to reach a state between being awake and being asleep. The brain starts to emit alpha waves, as it does during deep sleep. At first, you should learn how to do the technique correctly with a

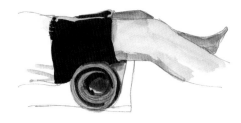

teacher but you will quickly be able to do it whenever and wherever you want. You will be able to hear noises around you while still in a state of inner rest. This technique teaches you to live in your body. When you've got the knack, this 'salutation to the sun' should be done every morning, and should be repeated four or five times.'

(note the illustrations of the postures: the candle pose, the crocodile, the beached fish, the salutation to the sun).

*The candle.*

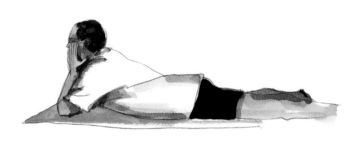

*The crocodile.*

*The beached fish.*

*The salutation to the sun.*

# 'The rise of the dragon',
## recharging your batteries

This foot massage, which requires a partner, was conceived by David Tran, a reflexologist. It recharges your batteries. 'It's the dragon which restores your energy,' says David Tran, but bear in mind that it also 'makes unfaithful husbands return.' The treatment takes about 15 minutes for each foot.

Sit with your legs stretched out in front of you and your feet facing your partner.
1 - The foot is kneaded with the thumb, from the bottom of the heel to the top. The pressure follows the median line of the foot to give you spiritual energy.
2 - 'The foot that says "no" is happy': with both hands, shake the foot in a seesaw motion from the ankles to the toes. This improves the circulation.
3 - Knead and massage the foot from the top to the diaphragm (see the foot map, p. 56). Use the fist to push and press, and pull and press.

*The benefits: an anti-stress special, this massage has no contra-indications and it will recharge your vital energy. At the end, you should feel fired with energy – the fire of the dragon.*

*Begin at the base of the foot and move upwards towards the toes, kneading with the thumb.*

*The foot that says 'no'.*

M O R E
STRESS

# Phytotherapy:
## using herbal infusions to relieve stress

We all know that mint infusions are popular after an over-heavy dinner. Still, it's the sort of thing that prim and proper old women go in for, don't you reckon? However, there are other infusions which have a carefully targeted effect on the body. According to Jean-Pierre Hubert, doctor, naturopathologist and sophrologist, 'what we eat is a factor in stress. Stress must be managed globally: food, life habits, sleep, transactional analysis or any other personal development method that helps you understand how we function.' But, for starters, here are some surprising treatments developed by people who believe in the power of plants to help the average, stressed out 30-year-old. You, maybe.

## The programme
### Detoxifying

You need to 'e-li-mi-nate' – flush out your emunctory organs (intestines, liver and skin) of toxins. Easy to use, quick acting, the infusion is ideal for the lazy. A sachet, some boiling water and there we have it. A cup of goodness, just for you. Our man has gone for a mixture of wild fig, sweet marjoram, lime and valerian. One spoonful of this mixture should be taken morning and night in boiling water.

## Moderating

Before adopting a new hygiene regime, cut out the obvious excesses and this will revitalise your body right from the word go. Let's go over it again: one coffee in the morning and that's all; sugar is fine but not refined sugar; rice and starchy foods, yes; vegetables, obviously; oily fish for omega 3; red meat – why not, but raw red meat is even better; not too much cheese, too rich. And finally, drink to excess. Water, of course. Although one glass of wine never did anyone any harm. Dr Jean-Pierre Hubert says, 'I'm not in favour of political correctness and draconian diets, but excesses and extremes will damage your health. You need to know how to treat your body well.'

## Relaxing

Mix up a special relaxation infusion from Dr Jean-Pierre Hubert. To a litre of water add 20 grams (one ounce) of the aerial part of the passion flower. Drink after every meal, especially in the evening.

## Choose your plants according to your needs

**Detoxifying:** artichoke, rosemary, balm-mint …
**Improving memory:** ginseng, hawthorn, passion flower …
**Stimulating:** star anise, ginseng, valerian …
**Regenerating:** thistle …
**Relaxing:** dioecious nettle, German camomile …
**Calming:** hawthorn, passion flower, thyme, balm-mint …
**Relieving depression:** St. John's Wort, rosemary …

*Good to know: in health shops you will find the following in capsules: borage oil to regenerate skin tissue, lecithin and pollen for memory, royal jelly (bought in pots) to boost the immune system and horsetail for minerals and vitality.*

## With your nose in the air

What is aromatherapy? It's part of our instinctive nature, where our sense of smell guides us as much as our eyes. Japanese researchers have shown that if you pump certain odours into the air on the underground, there are less aggressive incidents. Bakeries understand the advantages of releasing enticing odours into the air to stimulate hunger. And you can recreate Zen surroundings at home. Scented candles, incense, oil burners that you fill with water and a few drops of aromatic essence … it's up to you. Lime, orange blossom, lavender, cedar oils, or Tibetan incense sticks all have the power to soothe and relax.

# NO
MORE
STRESS

**30 mins**

## Shall I have a power up?

Stop saying, 'I'm going for a quick nap', and start saying, 'I'm going for a power-up.' This is a concept that originated in the US and has been recognised as beneficial by American researchers at the National Institute of Mental Health. Because of this, the nap has become an acceptable thing to do, even during office hours. In Basel in Switzerland, they have an ultra-trendy barge, christened 'the sleep boat'. It has luxurious cabins with comfy mattresses and duvets, and overworked professionals can go and rest for half an hour. The same concept can be found in Zurich, where there are rooms where you can rest for 20 minutes, between midday and 2 pm, for £2.50. In Paris, you can laze around in a very futuristic atmosphere in the new Kenzo Spa, and the stressed worker can grab forty winks, no appointment necessary. It costs £10 for half an hour in beautiful surroundings with a good mattress and a gentle awakening. 'Impossible to leave', we are assured. For those who don't have that sort of cash, the good old quick nap, favoured by Napoleon, is completely free of charge and remains in vogue.

*Rosemary*

*Thistle*

*Camomile*

*Thyme*

# When the pupil is

# ready ...

So, have you successfully tested all our SOS anti-stress tips and postures? The corpse pose, Dr Schültz's relaxation techniques, the benefits of infusions – these are no longer mysteries to you? Have you now realised that 'if you pull on the rope, it snaps'? Have you accepted that you will be ruled by your emotions if you deny their existence or give in to them? Now is the time to get down to the serious business and to really take matters in hand. From the jungle of techniques out there, we have researched, tested and then selected the best and the easiest activities, the ones that offer the optimum balance between pleasure and effectiveness. It's up to you to choose – taking into account your schedule and how much you want to change – from a range of techniques that are good for your senses, good for your overall wellbeing and the best for your body. There is a saying in yoga: 'when the pupil is ready, the master comes.'

# Have you got a week?

**If you are thinking, 'I've had enough of this exercise torture! I want something nice', let's get straight down to the massage parlour. The success of spa centres – places of luxury, calm and sensual pleasure – is not a matter of luck. Looks are not important; they pander to your need for enlightenment, your need for inner peace, rest, relaxation, pleasure and meditation.**

And what is the most fundamental thing they offer? The rediscovery of a sensual pleasure, a long-forgotten art that modern society has lost: the art of touch. Massage, so commonplace in Asian society because it is a part of family life from a very young age, is, for many, only associated with erotic pleasures and sex. This a huge macho, Western mistake. The action of touching to soothe pain is a basic human instinct. These days you go for a massage to get back to the basic fact that you are first and foremost a body. 'You get contact, an exchange, a tuning-in', adds Jean-François de Righetti, relaxologist, 'everything that modern life – obsessed with speed and performance – deprives us of'. As well as the feeling of wellbeing that touch gives us, the Chinese invented therapeutic massages over 4,500 years ago. These are based on the belief in the breath of life, qi (pronounced chi). Man is a cosmic element, between the sky (the head) and the earth (the feet), with his own energy balance. If your qi is blocked, there is an imbalance in your body. This belief is the foundation of a number of therapies including acupuncture, reflexology, shiatsu, Do-in and others.

## LaBulleKenzo Spa (Paris, France):

A whole programme, a menu of healing touches to choose from. When you emerge you will feel 'fulfilled', 'intoxicated', 'free from care', 'comforted and soothed', 'sensually drunk', 'illuminated' ... Where massage satisfies body and soul.

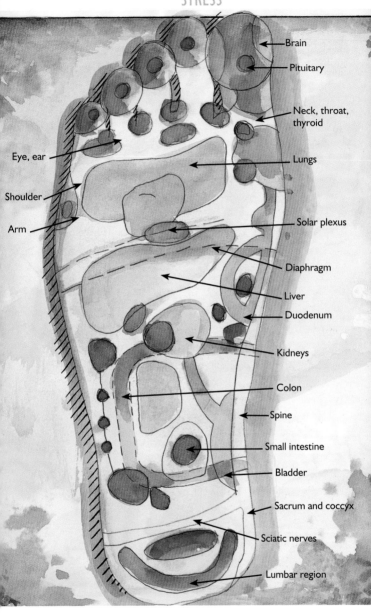

Brain

Pituitary

Neck, throat, thyroid

Eye, ear

Lungs

Shoulder

Arm

Solar plexus

Diaphragm

Liver

Duodenum

Kidneys

Colon

Spine

Small intestine

Bladder

Sacrum and coccyx

Sciatic nerves

Lumbar region

*The map of the right foot according to the Chinese tradition of reflexology.*

# Reflexology:
## how your foot reflects your whole body

Reflexology, a treatment carried out on the base of the feet, is based on the principles of traditional Chinese medicine. It is believed that each part of the foot reflects parts of your body and is based on the theory of vital energy. Reflexology is a holistic therapy that involves treating you as a whole – mind, body and spirit. The reflexologist is not concerned with the symptoms but tries to cure the cause of the problem. This technique aims to improve the flow of qi (pronounced 'chi') and to rebalance the qi in all areas of the body in order to find a vital harmony. The ultimate aim is to boost your body's natural defences. This therapy is usually especially effective for problems related to stress (backache, poor circulation, bowel disorders and insomnia). You will be able to soothe an uncomfortable symptom in one session, but you will need at least a further two sessions to treat the underlying problem and even more if you are trying to change a long-term habit, such as smoking or taking sleeping tablets.

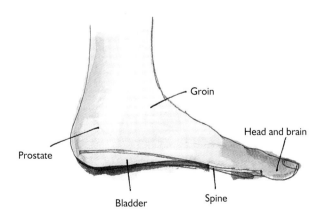

## NO
M O R E
STRESS

### *What's a session like?*

Once you have taken your shoes off, you sit in a relaxation chair, with your feet facing the reflexologist. The first session will be an assessment. Don't panic if you tell the reflexologist that you are feeling listless and he assures you that you have liver fatigue. When he or she presses on the reflex point concerned, you will see your foot in a whole new light. Reflexology works on the acupuncture points of the feet, by pressing, stroking or kneading with the fingers. It's about releasing negative emotions and redistributing them harmoniously throughout the body. The touch feels disarming: although you can only feel a gentle caress, the reflexologist is actually pressing firmly. In general, more sessions will be needed to complete the treatment.

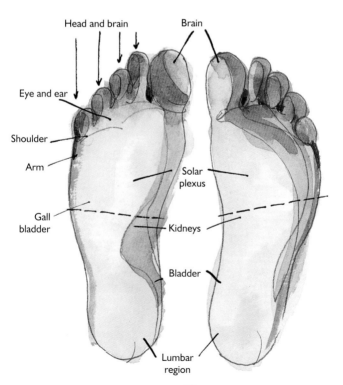

Head and brain

Brain

Eye and ear

Shoulder

Arm

Solar
plexus

Gall
bladder

Kidneys

Bladder

Lumbar
region

**How you feel afterwards:** light-headed and relaxed if you were feeling tense. Energised if you were feeling tired.

**Duration:** between 45 minutes and an hour.

*The benefits: particularly effective for stress-related problems such as back-ache, insomnia, bowel problems and circulatory problems. It can be used as part of a programme to quit smoking or simply as an escape from the daily grind. Excellent before an important deadline.*

## 'Transform your negative energy into productive energy'.

*David Tran, reflexologist, President of the Franco-Chinese Institute of Reflexology, a member of the French Reflexology Federation.*

'Acute stress can be transformed into productive and positive energy. Conversely, for people affected by chronic stress, the reflexologist will effectively be able to wipe the slate clean and reprogramme the body to stop it malfunctioning. For this, you need between three and five sessions in order to refine the treatment. Then the patient should have one session a week as maintenance. This also has a preventative effect because it boosts the immune system.'

# Shiatsu:
## getting in tune with your body

*What's a session like?*

Whether you are at home or in a centre, you should be dressed comfortably, with no shoes, lying on a tatami mat. You choose to lie on your back or your front. Shiatsuchi know that the part of the body 'offered' to the practitioner will instinctively be the one that feels bad. 'Except that men tend to offer their backs. This is a defensive impulse which they have difficulty resisting,' says Tatiana Vaes, shiatsuchi. 'Apart from the fact that the back is a place where tensions tend to build up, touch is intimate and it can scare men to offer their stomachs, which are more vulnerable.' Shiatsu uses many of the same principles as reflexology: you stimulate the parts in which there is a lack of energy and release those areas where there is too much. The shiatsuchi starts by stretching the body, then uses firm finger pressure, muscular massages and strokes, and also works, on sensitive points using the whole weight of his or her body. After he or she has worked along the meridians of the legs and the feet, a session is completed with a head massage.

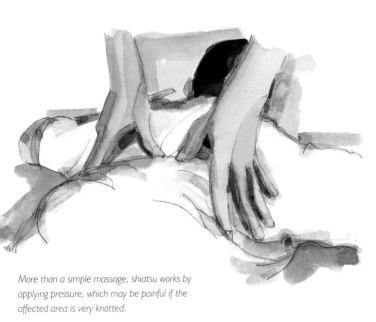

*More than a simple massage, shiatsu works by
applying pressure, which may be painful if the
affected area is very knotted.*

*All the meridians of the body are massaged during
a shiatsu session. The aim is to make energy flow
around the body without any blockages.*

week

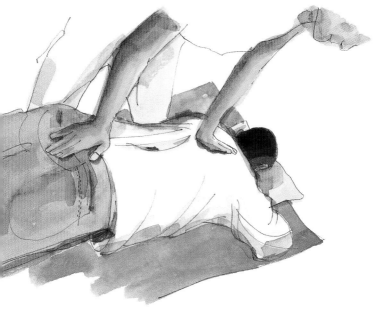

*Stretches, pressure, kneading and light
massage all make up the technique of shiatsu.*

**How you feel afterwards:** your body is completely relaxed, your mind is clear and calm and, outside, it feels as if there is a protective barrier between you and reality.

**Duration:** an hour to an hour and a half.

***The benefits:*** *this technique works on the causes rather than the symptoms of stress, so it has no immediate effect except a feeling of wellbeing (don't schedule a brainstorming meeting after a session!) You need to wait a few days for results. For those not just interested in quick-fix solutions, a more long-term programme is advised. You will learn to recentre yourself and practise the art of 'letting go'. 'You need to be in control of yourself and shiatsu helps you get in tune with your body,' says Tatiana. But, gentlemen, you have to be prepared to be touched, without getting tense or laughing nervously, and you have to let yourself be massaged by the shiatsuchi (who will be on top of you) without thinking that she is coming on to you.*

### 'Before an important decision'
*Bertrand, 30, photographer.*

'I'm pretty sporty. I play tennis and I go jogging, which I find are useful ways of letting myself go. But I have become a fan of this technique because it makes me feel fantastic. The first time I had shiatsu, I was surprised. I was expecting a massage. In fact, it's all about applying pressure so it can even sometimes be painful. It's about making time for yourself – and there is no competition. I would recommend having a shiatsu session before making important decisions.'

# Ayurvedic massage:
## soothing stress

*What's a session like?*

It's an Indian version of a therapeutic Chinese massage, with sensual pleasure thrown in. Ayurveda (from ayur, 'science, art'; and veda, 'life') is a traditional Indian science based on vital energy. It is a preventative technique, more of a way of life. The aim is to balance your body's energy.

In this technique, energy is known as prana and the practitioner makes energy levels go up or down, depending on the patient's needs. 'Everyone is controlled by the five elements (air, fire, water, earth and ether) and each element is linked to precise organs in the body,' says Sandrine from the Tapovan Massage Centre in Paris.

The practitioner uses ayurvedic oil, specially chosen to suit you. Wearing your underwear and covered with a massage towel, you will be given an abyanga, a body massage which relieves tension in what are known as the four stress points: the back (daily stress), the stomach (jealousy), the chest (negative emotions) and the gluteal muscles (stress from sitting). In a pleasant atmosphere, in silence and with incense (its smell will relax you), you will be treated to a massage that will please and soothe your senses.

**How you feel afterwards:** relaxed, as if 'the whole world is filled with love'.

**Duration:** only 50 minutes.

*The benefits: after the first session you will want to make an appointment for the next day, there and then. But the drawback of this ecstatic feeling, we must admit, is that the effects wear off pretty quickly during the course of the following day. But you'll want to feel that way again so you'll hurry back anyway. 'The ideal thing to do,' according to Sandrine, 'is to start with three massages to rebalance the body and then have one a month to keep it up.'*

# Kansu: copper bowl massage

Equipped with a copper bowl (kansu) and ghee (clarified butter) the practitioner smears the butter over the soles of the feet and then glides the base of the bowl over them. This technique balances the 'fire' of the body thanks to the alchemy of the copper and the ghee. It's designed to fight stress. After 20 minutes on each sole, the treatment is completed with a little foot massage.

## Have you got a month?

You are on the verge of a new beginning. At this stage, you have become aware of imbalances in your life and what you want from now on. You want renewal, a break from the way you functioned in the past.

You need to take yourself in hand. We are not talking miracle cures but simple changes of direction. You know what you want to change: you may want to stop smoking, to sleep well, go fishing, feel physically fitter, improve your relationships, manage your emotions, resolve your work

 problems, talk to your partner. And now you know how to do it: to (re)find yourself, learn to control and release your feelings, build up a new life force. Warning, major works ahead!

# Sport, oxygen for the soul
## Three-stage programme to get yourself back into shape

You think you understand all the benefits of sport? A good old game of squash, build up a good sweat and then you're ready to roll again? Typical male mistake! When you are tense, you should avoid aggressive sports: they add tension to the body where it is already in pain. And tension + tension = nothing for the body.

1) **Check-up:** for sedentary and inactive people, it is important to visit your doctor for a check-up, to make sure that playing sport is safe for you. In a cardiology centre, you will be hooked up to a machine that will measure your heart rate. This test is particularly important for men who did plenty of sport when they were younger and who now, after a break of several years, think they can still perform like a 20-year-old just because they have a new tracksuit and a 40-gear bike.

**2) Go gradually:** start gently, in terms of duration and intensity. At first, 15 or 20 minutes is enough, you should take care to stretch properly before and after. Exercise should be done three times a week rather than three hours all in one go! Take your pulse at the end of the session. If you are between the ages of 30 and 45, your pulse should be around 150 beats a minute.

**3) Increase the duration:** 25 or 30 minutes, two or three times a week. In general your resting heart rate should be lower than when you started.

*The benefits: normally, after a month of this regime, you will start to notice the benefits. Your body should become more muscular and toned, and your respiratory capacity should increase. Physical exercise is an ideal way to 'clear your head'. Don't make the mistake of thinking it's easy: you will not start producing endorphins, the famous 'happiness molecules' that sporty people talk about, after 30 minutes of gentle jogging. According to specialists, this precious hormone is produced only when physical effort is maintained over many hours. In a half-marathon for example ... however, this weekly session will mean that the body is drained and oxygenated. This is the effect you are looking for.*

## 'I feel free on my bike'

*Hervé, 38, Senior Civil Servant.*

'As I am cooped up for the whole day from 9am to 11pm, I decided to cycle to work. It's a way of keeping me sane and it has changed my life. I burn off physical energy and above all I feel I am free and in control; to go where I want, when I want, away from any traffic jams. During the journey, I switch off, both metaphorically and literally.'

**NO** MORE STRESS

## 'Put endurance sports first'

*Dr Frederic Taousse, doctor to the French athletics team.*

'When you do endurance sports, your aerobic metabolism kicks in. Your muscles use oxygen and sugar as fuel. The body will therefore use up all its store of sugar before getting its energy from fats. That's why sport is better for a healthy life than as a means of losing weight. Swimming, jogging and cycling are three endurance sports you should try first because they are good for the heart. Water supports the body so swimming allows your muscles to work without stress on the joints. Front crawl stretches and works the whole body. Jogging tones up your thighs and buttocks and your quadriceps but can harm your joints. Cycling is the least stressful activity for your joints, and gets your quadriceps and arms working. But the best exercise in my opinion is rowing, which we tend to forget. You are sitting down, which does not harm the joints, and you work your back, thighs and arms.'

NO
M O R E
STRESS

## 'Martial arts for energy'

*Patrick, 41, is a soldier, formerly responsible within special forces.*

'All soldiers have to be physically fit. When I was in my unit, on the ground, I was doing two hours of sport a day. I did lots of combat sports, self-defence, boxing and karate. On top of this, I did mountain-biking, swimming and rope climbing. It was a way of forgetting my work and personal tensions, a way of channelling my energy. But this permanent training also enabled us to adapt, when we went on operations, to all sorts of situations that were stressful by definition and so we were in a good position to deal with that stress. Today, I would say that martial arts taught me how to let myself go and also how to recharge myself.'

# Qi Gong:
## calm energy

Some people describe this as gymnastics for your energy levels. For Yves Réquéna, a Qi Gong (pronounced 'Chi Kong') teacher, it is, like yoga, 'a gymnastic art with movements that combine the opposite principles of yin and yang. It's a slow dance and the aim is to give you additional vital energy and to get it circulating around the body along the acupuncture meridian lines. It's also about not letting yourself be hampered by your emotions and arriving at a state of "calm energy". There are thousands of qualified practitioners, with sessions being carried out in companies and in schools; in dancing, singing and martial arts classes.'

## What's a session like?

Dressed in comfortable clothes, you warm up your joints slowly, carefully monitoring how they feel. Then you start doing movements with sing-song names: 'the phoenix spreads his wings'; 'the purple swallow flies high in the sky'; 'tiger meets dragon'; 'the eagle opens his wings' … it's not about physical strength but endurance. 'I work with professional footballers, true athletes who simply cannot hold a posture for half an hour,' says Yves Réquéna. You finish by breathing through the stomach, the home of your vital energy. According to a qi master, you should feel a fireball in your lower belly or a light between your eyebrows: this shows the increase in energy levels. Fantastic!

**How do you feel afterwards:** physically and mentally relaxed. You feel like you are really living in your body; your breathing is gentle, your movements are deliberate. You are in control of your emotions. You set off a bit slower on the treadmill of life.

**Duration:** one hour

*The benefits: an excellent anti-stress measure. Eventually, according to our Qi Gong master, the goal is to reach a state of enlightenment where you have mastered your body and your energy flows without any special intellectual effort. After several sessions, your energy levels, your ability to recover physically, your concentration and, for some, your sexual energy, are increased by a factor of 10.*

# Anti-stress courses:
## soothing your mind

There are hundreds of these courses today, whether they specialise in stress management at work, or take a personal development approach like at the Dojo. They offer a range of courses that run from a few days to a week, or even one-to-one support that runs over several months. It is up to the individual to choose the method, but all these courses are based on psychological, relaxation or communication techniques and they often combine one with the other: sophrology, PNL (neurolinguistic programming), transactional analysis, behavioural and cognitive therapy, hypnosis. A list of rather intimidating names to which we have been able to add 'life coaching', which developed at the end of the 1990s.

# Therapy or personal development?

This is the crux of the problem; the border between these two schools of thought is blurred. The threshold of 'therapy' is quickly crossed, whether it be curing an anxiety by suggesting different behaviour or by helping someone understand it more clearly. This guide stops where psychotherapy and psychoanalysis start.

# What you will learn:

Courses usually work on resolving specific issues: public speaking, managing emotions, negotiating, learning how to say no, expressing your anger, conflict management, working on your emotional dynamic, to name but a few. Using the techniques over a long period of time can bring a better understanding of yourself. But do not ask the impossible: if you feel like killing your father, want to break your bond with your mother, or if you feel really depressed, you need to visit a psychologist, or look into psychotherapy or psychoanalysis.

To help you find your way, here is a general survey of the techniques that can help you. They have been proven to work on specific symptoms and on clear needs. It is difficult at this stage to put one method over another, since everything depends on the relationship you strike up with your mentor or 'personal developer'.

**NO** M O R E **STRESS**

## 'Men have forgotten how to feel'

*Aliette de Panafieu, psychotherapist.*

'In my company, which deals with the business of life, I work with groups on anger management. At the request of some of my groups, I set up a group on rage for men. I found that men were victims of cultural stereotypes and that they were not able to express their feelings as easily as women. Essentially, men have forgotten how to feel. They do not allow themselves to cry, and are inhibited by loads of things they can't do, especially expressing themselves. The principle of the group was to accept this rage, to let it surface and then to get through it. Sessions start at 8pm on Friday evening and finish on Saturday evening at the same time. For 24

hours non-stop, they follow the path I offer them. At the start there is a lot of resistance, but when they get more physically tired, psychological barriers begin to drop. For example, I have a session where they can express their rage by whacking a mattress with a racket. With this group I emphasise the feeling of belonging because this is something men lack. I tell them to assert themselves, to let their aggression go. As soon as aggression is expressed in words it becomes a moving energy. But if rage is not expressed, it turns into violence. At the end, their faces have changed, they sleep better and they have re-organised their priorities. You can change and become more self-confident, but you have to accept the price, which is human contact and being prepared to commit for a period of time.'

# PNL: positive communication

'A way of modelling human behaviour', according to Jane Turner, didactic psychotherapist in PNL.

**The benefits**: *this communication tool enables you to deprogramme problematic behaviour and reprogramme it to overcome your problems. If you have communication problems, PNL enables you to connect with the person you are speaking to and get in tune with them.*

# Know how to say 'no'

This forms the basis of all anti-stress strategy. This exercise is part of the sessions given at courses run by Gérard Vasselin, training consultant and specialist in PNL. Transactional analysis and sophro-relaxation enable participants to work on assertiveness, which builds up self-affirmation. The ability to say 'no' is the foundation. You learn how to resist pressure:

1/ **The broken record:** when you are harrassed by a sales rep, refuse clearly and in a neutral tone: 'I understand very well but it is not possible / I do not want to / I am not interested'. Repeat this, staying calm and using the same tone, rather like a broken record.

2/ **Passive agreement:** when you are accused of something, criticised or blamed for something with good reason, you should say, 'that's exactly right / that's true / that's entirely possible', without attempting to justify yourself.

3/ **Caught in the crossfire:** speaking privately with someone, you should formulate your disagreement with him immediately: state it clearly and follow it up with a clear request. The principle is to disassociate the blame (object) from the person you are talking to (personal).

*Example: a departmental head takes advantage of the kindness of one of his colleagues:*
*- 'You have asked me this many times (the facts). This annoys me because (how I feel, what this provokes in me) ... Could you in the future ... (a clear request) ... to maintain our good relations (finish on a positive note).*

## Sophrology: breathe usefully

This is a technique that will help you to be positive about events, to manage stressful situations such as overwork and anxiety by using breathing exercises and visualisation. It is often used by doctors.

**Duration:** one hour.

*The benefits: a short therapy, between three and five sessions, to cure a specific problem.*

## Transactional analysis: get to the sources of stress

This is a technique which enables you to identify which stresses have external (environmental) causes and which are internal (psychological). This work is undertaken with a trainer who helps you to decipher your personal programming, which has developed since your childhood and which may be the root cause of your problems. This helps you to learn to differentiate between you as a parent, you as a child and you as an adult.

*The benefits: this self-diagnostic exercise enables you to correct negative patterns of behaviour.*

## Hypnosis: unblock the unconscious

This technique, modified to combat psychosomatic problems, works on your behaviour. 'This can help the subject to change patterns of behaviour,' according to Jane Turner at the Dojo. Hypnosis can be effective for physiological habits (stopping smoking) and psychological habits (exploring the unconscious).

**The benefits:** *you do not need many sessions to get a result.*

# Identify your parental influences

This is one of the transactional analysis exercises offered by Gérard Vasselin: 'Messages instilled in us by our parents often build up in an inhibiting way, giving us attributes which explain our adult behaviour. The idea is to become aware of how they build up stress in us'. Can you identify the messages you got from your parents in these patterns of behaviour?

- **I can never rely on you; you're just not reliable!**
  → You will invariably feel you have failed in his aims.

- **Hurry up!**
  → You will constantly be racing against the clock.

- **Be perfect!**
  → You will put enormous pressure on yourself to succeed.

- **Be strong!**
  → You will make it a point of honour to sort things out all on your own, gritting your teeth and coping.

- **Make me happy!**
  → You will not be able to say 'no'; you are too eager to please.

- **Make an effort!**
  → You will use up all your energy on a task in the belief that you have to do it until your eyes pop with the effort. So you work endlessly.

# Non violent communication (NVC)

This method of communication, invented by Marshall Rosenberg, defines two types of communication: 'jackal language' and 'giraffe language'. The jackal barks, howls, judges, creates conflict, manipulates. The giraffe speaks quietly, openly, observes without judgement, expresses his feelings without making others responsible for his misfortunes. Learning this technique enables you to defuse verbal aggression and to formulate authentic requests.

## Learn giraffe language

### Note the difference between the jackal, who:

- **Judges:** 'You're an idiot'
- **Blames himself:** 'I'm rubbish'
- **Blackmails:** 'If you don't do this ...'
- **Blames others and sets up a power relationship:** 'What, you mean you didn't know that?'

### and the giraffe, who:

- **Puts things into perspective:** 'I was wrong, it happens to everyone'
- **Does not accuse:** 'I've got the feeling that ...'
- **Expresses his feelings:** 'When you said that ... I felt ...'
- **Does not impose himself but offers choices:** 'How do you see this? In what way?'

*I was wrong, it happens to everyone …*

**The benefits:** NVC enables you to be clear in your behaviour, in what you want and what you say. It allows you to listen actively and reformulate the words of others. But above all it allows you to defuse and transform aggression and anger in order to manage conflict by enabling all parties to feel satisfied. You learn how to say 'no', how to accept someone else saying 'no' and how to break the silence. In short, it reduces stress in your dealings with others.

## Practise verbal aikido

This communication technique takes its inspiration from Asian martial arts and allows you to use the aggression of another person against them. 'When they push, pull; and when they pull, push,' says Gérard Vasselin. If you are attacked, accept it at first (don't react instantly with an immediate counter-attack), reorientate, then assert.

*Examples:*

* **A colleague in a meeting says:** 'Your project will never work.'

   ➜ **The aikido response:** 'Well sure, it's not 100 per cent guaranteed to work. What do you suggest?'

* **'You women are all the same!'**

   ➜ **The aikido response:** 'Well, thank you for noticing. Now that we've cleared that up, is it a problem?'

* **'You're too young to understand.'**

   ➜ **The aikido response:** 'Well, of course, I can't be older than my age. Could you explain it to me?'

* **'That's unacceptable, you are useless!'**

   ➜ **The aikido response:** 'Have you decided to sack me immediately, sir, or will you give me a second chance?'

# Coaching: a friend to help you

Coaching could be defined as support and assistance for people or teams to develop their potential and their skills within the framework of professional or private objectives. Many companies have turned to a coach to optimise the potential of their directors and their teams.

Coaching responds to a specific desire to change behaviour or to learn basic life skills that have been lost in the rush for personal success. We tackle everything from 'managing your team at work' to life goals, or succeeding in forming a meaningful relationship. Personal or life coaching has a bright future.

## *What's a session like?*

'We assess each person to identify his needs,' says Jane Turner. 'After two or three sessions, we have defined a goal and a strategy to achieve that goal.' Coaching ends when the subject has reached his or her goal, which can take time.

**The benefits:** *in concrete terms, this approach is quick and it is targeted specifically to your needs. Therapeutic work, if it is necessary, depends on how experienced the coach is. 'With coaching, you acquire a new direction in your life,' says Jane Turner.*

# cool

# Conclusion

So, are you happy? For the first time, we are addressing this question to you. This guide has aimed to be your travelling companion on the road to increased wellbeing. If, after all the help and guidance you have been offered, you say 'yes', this guide will have helped you see that wellbeing is within reach and you will understand that there is nothing worse than bottling up frustrations and anger. So, express yourself – express your frustrations. There are a thousand ways to do it. On the other hand, you may still feel this isn't right for you. You may still think that being good to yourself makes you less of a man, or that 'discussing your problems' is fine for women. If this is so, be aware that, according to a recent study, the risk of cardiovascular disease is three times higher in people who bottle things up. That's got to be worth thinking about, surely?

# Further information

www.who.int (World Health
Organisation)

www.isma.org.uk (International Stress
Management Association)

www.stressmanagement.co.uk (Stress
Management Co. UK)

www.howtomanagestress.co.uk

www.stress-counselling.co.uk

## FEDERATIONS

Yoga: www.yogauk.com

Reflexology: www.reflexology.org

Shiatsu: www.shiatsu.org (Shiatsu
Society UK)

Sophrology:
www.sophrology.therapies-uk.com

Qi gong: www.qimagazine.co.uk (Tse
Qu Gong Centre)

Non violent communication (NCV):
www.acnv.com

## BOOKS

*The Complete Idiot's Guide to Managing
Stress*, Jeff Davidson, Alpha Books,
1999.

*Manage Your Mind: Mental Fitness
Guide*, Gillian Butler and Tony Hope,
Oxford Paperbacks, 1995.

*The Complete Idiot's Guide to Tai Chi
and Quigong*, Bill Douglas, Alpha Books,
2002.

*Therapeutic Yoga*, Mosaraf Ali and Jiwan
Brar, Vermilion, 2002.

*Shiatsu: The Complete Guide*,
Chris Jarmey and Gabriel Mojay,
HarperCollins, 1999.

*The Reflexology Handbook: A Complete
Guide*, Laura Norman et al, Piatkus
Books, 2004.

# Acknowledgements

**This guide would not have had the same flavour if I had not been helped by individuals who gave as much of themselves as of their advice:**

Thanks to the unfailing availability of David Tran, reflexologist (President of the Franco-Chinese Reflexology Institute and member of the French Reflexology Federation).

To the generosity of Jean-François de Righetti, relaxologist and yoga master.

To the kindness of the shiatsuchi of the FFST.

To the enthusiasm of Yves Réquéna, qi gong master at the French Federation.

To the co-operative spirit of Gérard Vasselin, teacher at the ARCC (Animation Research Communication Council) training office.

To the goodwill of Dr Jean-Pierre Hubert, naturopathologist.

And to Jane Turner, didactic psychotherapist in PNL and Ericksonian hypnosis, coach at the Dojo, member of the French Federation of Personal Development.

Thanks also to all those stressed-out people who helped themselves and who were then prepared to share their experience in the spirit of solidarity, taking up their precious personal and family time.

Finally, thanks to Alain Bouldouyre, famous illustrator, a cheerful guinea pig and recent convert, who enabled me to get an accurate picture of the resistance and scepticism of men when it comes to their wellbeing.